THE SWEETNESS OF LIFE

I gratefully acknowledge the financial support of the Foundation for Yiddish Culture.

The Sweetness of Life © 2018

Cover design: Cheryl Everett Rajchgot

Library and Archives Canada Cataloguing in Publication

Rajchgot, Harry, author

    The sweetness of life / Harry Rajchgot

Paperback edition   ISBN 978-0-9950435-2-7

Amazon ebook edition   ISBN 978-0-9950435-3-4

bodsanow books

Montreal, Quebec, Canada

www.gravitationalfields.com

The Sweetness of Life

די זיסקייַט פֿון לעבן

My Mother's Yiddish Cookbook

Also by HARRY RAJCHGOT

Gravitational Fields, A Novel of Peacetime and War

Purimspiel! Original Purimspiel Plays (with Rabbi Leigh Lerner)

Both are available on Amazon.ca in print and ebook versions.

CONTENTS

Maybe you speak Yiddish, once spoke Yiddish, or would like to learn Yiddish.
Maybe you cook, once cooked, or would like to cook.

Maybe you have a mother, had a mother, or would like to have a mother.

If any of these apply, this is the book for you.

My mother would have said so.

Believe me.

אַײנפֿירען

איך שרײַב דאָ עטלעכע ווערטער צו דאַנקען די אונטערשטיצערס פֿון דער
פֿונדאַציע פֿאַר ייִדישער קולטור. איך האָב פּראָבירט דאָ ווײַזן די געשיכטע פֿון
מײַנע משפּחה און אונדזער וואַנדערונג פֿון פּוילן פֿאַר דער צווייטער וועלט
מלחמה ביז אונדזער אימיגראַציע קיין מאַנטריאַל. איך האָב געשריבן וועגן דער
וואָקס פֿון ייִדיש פֿון די צײַט פֿון די ערשטע ייִדן אין מזרח אייראָפּע.

דאָס איז אויך אַ בוך וועגן ייִדישע עסנוואַרג, און אויך וועגן משפּחה און
פֿרײַנדשאַפֿט. עס דערצײַלט וועגן די געזעלשאַפֿט וואָס די מענער און פֿרויען
האָבן דאָ באַשאַפֿן נאָך דעם חורבן און זײַנער אַלטע וועלט, און ווי אַזוי דאָס
לעבן איז געגאַנגען פֿאַרויס און גייט נאָך אַלץ פֿאַרויס.

טראַדיציעס האָבן זיך געענדערט, אָבער זיי לעבן מיט אונדז פֿון איין דור צום
אַנדערן. יעדער דור נעמט די מתנה און מאַכט עס איבער, ווי אַמאָל האָט מען
עס ארויסגעוואָרפֿן, ווי אַמאָל אַדאַפּטירט. דאָס איז די געשיכטע פֿון דעם
המשך, פֿון ליבשאַפֿט, פֿון לעבן, און די נאַטירלעכע פֿאַרבינדונג צווישן מאַלצײַט
און היימישן טיש.

Introduction

This is not meant to be a scholarly book. Nor a history book. Nor a recipe book. But it's all of those.

It's not a thorough attempt to explain where Yiddish came from, although there is some of that. It's not an analysis of the similarities between Yiddish and other related European languages, although there is some of that. It's not about the different forms of Yiddish in Eastern and Western Europe, or between Lithuanian scholarly Yiddish (Standard Yiddish) and the Yiddish of the shtetls of Poland, although there is some of that, too.

It's not a comprehensive listing of recipes for the variety of food eaten in Jewish homes in Poland, which is where my mother was born and lived until 1939. It's not a thorough history lesson, nor is it even a thorough biography. Yet it is all of these.

What I hope it is, is a tale about my parents, especially my mother, where they came from, how they came to arrive in Canada, and how they made the best of what they had, the life force that drove them, the culture and language they grew up with and knew, used, and often celebrated in, and how they built their, and my and my brother's lives, here in Montreal. It speaks of Yiddish, food, and life.

My parents' language of the home was Yiddish. The Yiddish my mother grew up with was not learned in academic study, but it was authentic, and the first language I learned as a young child, before I went to school and learned English. I have written here a history of my parents, from their origins in pre-war Poland until the German invasion that started the Second World War disrupted and almost took their lives, and which did take those of countless European Jews, and from then onward to Canada.

After the war, they arrived in Montreal. They were fluent in a number of other languages—Polish, Russian, and German. They were able to write their Polish using the modified Roman alphabet of the Poles, and their Russian in the Cyrillic alphabet, but in their home and in their community, they spoke Yiddish and wrote it with the Hebrew *aleph beit* (the Yiddish *alef beis.*). They brought their

Yiddish to Canada with them. So had many of the Jews of Eastern Europe who arrived in North America in several waves of immigration, beginning in the the late nineteenth century, culminating in the arrival after the Second World War of survivors of the Holocaust.

Jews arrived in Eastern Europe in large numbers a thousand years ago, driven out of other parts of Europe during the First Crusade. They moved from the remains of the Roman Empire after its fall, into the areas that later became early France, then to the German principalities, and from there they continued eastwards. Along the way, they adopted the local languages, and modified these for their domestic use by adding in bits of Hebrew and Aramaic. Yiddish developed. Boreslaw III, the King of Poland about a thousand years ago, saw the Jews as a people who would bring commerce and modernization with them, and encouraged them to settle in his lands. Over the next centuries, Yiddish grew as a mingling German and Hebrew, and it became the language of the Jewish *shtetls* in the Polish lands. Ultimately, Poland in its many drifting parts (at certain times encompassing Lithuania, Ukraine, and Belarus) became the home to the largest Jewish contingent in Europe , and in the world. The Jews lived in these small towns for a thousand years until modern times began to change things, bring in new ideas about The Enlightenment, the brotherhood of man, the bankruptcy of the aristocracy and its way of life, freedom of thought, freedom of religion, and the equality of all men. It also brought a resurgence of what had been a medieval antisemitism, and with it pogroms, repression, forced long-term conscription, expulsions, and this led to a mass emigration to North America by Jews, growing in size during the later decades of the nineteenth century and the early twentieth. These emigrant Jews were the fortunate ones, leaving their old world behind because of circumstance, foresight, or luck. They got out when it was still possible to do that.

My parents weren't among these early emigrants. My grandparents were born in Poland, and stayed in Poland. Their children also stayed, until it was too late.

א אָ ב בֿ ב ג ד ה ו וו וֹי ח ט י יי ײַ כ כ ך ל מ ם נ ן ס ע פ פֿ פ ף צ ץ ק ר ש ש ת ת

The Past, A Little Yiddish, and Some Jewish Cooking

1435 ST. ALEXANDER STREET
SUITE 615

SALES TAX EXTRA

York Fur Inc.

MANUFACTURERS OF FINE FURS

Montreal, Que. H3A 2G4 _____ 197____

Shipped To: _____
Address _____
City _____

DATE

DEPT. No.

OUR ORDER No.

YOUR ORDER No.

TERMS

VIA

STOCK No.	STYLE	QTY.	DESCRIPTION	PRICE	TOTAL

NO CLAIMS ALLOWED AFTER 5 DAYS FROM RECEIPT OF GOODS

SHIPPING MEMO

Nº 3951

10

Cheese cake (Cheese Johnnycake)

from Mrs. Goldman
(Djani Kaich)

Oven at 375°, 1.5 hrs.

1 glass regular flour
1 glass corn flour
1 glass sugar
2 teaspoons baking powder
1/4 margarine
2 glasses milk
3 eggs
1 pint cottage cheese

Mix together all 4 ingredients. Afterwards add in the butter. Put in the milk. When all is mixed together, we put in the eggs.

Put the cottage cheese in the middle of the cake before baking the cake.

But now that we've lamented the past, as for all our festivals of freedom, let's get on with the food. Let's eat! There are recipes in this book for cooking Jewish food, yet there is more to them than just being a set of recipes, although, as we say at Passover, *dayenu*, it would have been enough, or, in Yiddish, גענוג (*genug.)*

Enough with the mourning; this isn't a funeral! Where's the food, already?

 Jewish food has always had its specificity and quirks and religious precepts, but this book is also about family and friendship, about the social circle of Jewish men and women that formed here in Montreal among survivors of the Holocaust. It describes how life went on, and goes on, how traditions, although changing and adapting over time, remain. They are part of us and how we see and live in the world. This is a book about transformation, how one generation passes on its culture to the next, and how that next generation takes that gift, changing it, sometimes rejecting it (oy vey!), other times loving it, and adding to it. It is a story of continuity, of love, family, life, friendship, and the sustaining gift of meals at the family table.

This is a "herstory", because it tells of friendships and family attachments among the Jewish women who came to Montreal with their families. More than that, this is the story of my family's origins and slow flourishing in Canada, and the history and culture of the food that was a central part of that journey.

This book is also, and perhaps primarily, a family and social history, and an exploration of a period of time–the years prior to World War II–and a particular place–Eastern Europe, specifically Poland–and the Jews who had inhabited that country at that time, who lived their own way amidst their Catholic neighbours. They had their own cuisine, their own religious and cultural practices, and their own language, Yiddish.

The recipes included are not all my mother's, but she wrote them down and used them. They were given to her by her circle of friends, other women who had lived similar lives. I came upon these recipes after her death. Each was written out on a scrap of paper or the piece of cardboard closure from a box of Kleenex, a cardboard reinforcement of a shirt returned from the dry cleaners, or on the back of a supermarket receipt, but mostly they were written down on the pages of an invoice book from one of the fur coat manufacturers that she worked for much of her life. Many have not been tested because of a paucity of details within, ambiguous instructions, and sometimes difficult to interpret hand-writing.

1435 ST. ALEXANDER STREET
SUITE 615

SALES TAX EXTRA

York Fur Inc.

MANUFACTURERS OF FINE FURS

Montreal, Que. H3A 2G4 _____ 197____

| DATE |
| DEPT. No. |
| OUR ORDER No. |
| YOUR ORDER No. |
| TERMS |
| VIA |

Shipped To: _____

Address _____

City _____

STOCK No.	STYLE	QTY.	DESCRIPTION	PRICE	TOTAL

NO CLAIMS ALLOWED AFTER 5 DAYS FROM RECEIPT OF GOODS

SHIPPING MEMO

Nº 3963

14

From Pearl Blumenkranc

Chocolate Cookies

4 eggs
1 glass sugar
1/2 package margarine
3 spoons baking powder
1 spoon oil
flour as much as it takes up (??)
1 package chocolate chips

Summer in Bodsanow, my father's town. My father is the closest figure in the water

My parents both came from small towns in Poland, my mother from Rozan, my father from Bodsanow. They were both brought up speaking Yiddish, although they were also fluent in Polish and had some understanding of Hebrew. Life before the war was never easy. More or less as Charles Dickens has so famously put it, it wasn't the best of times, but it wasn't the worst of times, either. It was a small town life, and Jews lived alongside their Polish neighbours, for better or for worse.

Harvest time in Bodsanow

When war arrived on their doorsteps in September of 1939, within a week or two of the German invasion of Poland that precipitated World War II, they had to leave. My father Frank (Froim) left straight away with a few friends, and crossed the border into Russia only days later, after failing to convince his family and his then girlfriend to go with him. They were all lost to the Holocaust in the years that followed. Ester, my mother, who was then 15 years old, was being cared for by her older sister Haya Leah. She had been orphaned at a young age, her father dying in the months before she was born, and her mother when Ester was still a child. She was pushed and pulled along the refugee roads towards the city of Bialystok, which sat on the Polish (Nazi-dominated) side of the new border between the extended German Reich and the enlarged Soviet Union. Poland as a country was gone. In Bialystok, she worked as a slave labourer, before she and her sister's family managed somehow to get across into the Soviet Union and temporary freedom from the danger of genocide, and found there a remarkable lack of anti-semitism. Russia was in turn invaded by the Nazis in 1941, and it was not until the spring of 1945 that the steady retreat of German forces back toward their no longer mighty Fatherland finally brought peace.

Unidentified family members in Poland, mostly lost in the war

TEL.: 844-3397
844-3398

1435 ST. ALEXANDER STREET
SUITE 615

York Fur Inc.

MANUFACTURERS OF FINE FURS

Montreal, Que. H3A 2G4 _____ 197___

Shipped To: _____

Address _____

City _____

SALES TAX EXTRA
DATE
DEPT. No.
OUR ORDER No.
YOUR ORDER No.
TERMS
VIA

STOCK No.	STYLE	QTY.	DESCRIPTION	PRICE	TOTAL

NO CLAIMS ALLOWED AFTER 5 DAYS FROM RECEIPT OF GOODS

SHIPPING MEMO

Nº 3962

Honey Cake

From Basha Teich

> 4 eggs
> 1 cup sugar
> 1 glass honey
> 3/4 glass oil
> 1 glass coffee
> 2 spoons baking powder
> 1/2 spoon baking soda
> 2 3/4 cups flour

Mix together the flour, the baking powder, and the baking soda. Mix together the flour with the baking powder in with the baking soda.

In the Soviet Union, the restrictions brought on by war made life severe. My mother's older sister had two young children when the war began. They lived in extreme deprivation, the threat of starvation and disease always there. My mother was for a time sent to a labour camp in the far North for becoming sick and not being able to report for work. Despite these many hardships, my parents eventually met and fell in love. In January 1946, with the the war finally over and my parents safe, they were married by a rabbi in what was then an illegal religious ceremony. Their hand-written *ketubah*–their Jewish marriage contract–is still with me.

בשבת בשבת שנ... נ.מים. לחדש .ש.ב.ג.ב שנת חמשת אלפים
ושבע מאות ושש שנים לבריאת עולם למנין שאנו
מנין כאן עיר טשעקאלאוו איך מוה'/ק... במו"ה בה:
... אמר להדא בתולתא מרת /... בת מו'ה :פי.
... הוי לי לאנתו כדת משה וישראל ואנא אפלח
ואוקיר ואיזון ואפרנס יתיכי ליכי כהלכות גוברין יהודאין
דפלחין ומוקרין וזנין ומפרנסין לנשיהון בקושטא ויהיבנא
ליכי מוהר בתוליכי כסף זוזי מאתן דחזו ליכי מדאורייתא
ומזונייכי ונסותייכי וספוקייכי ומיעל לותיכי כאורח כל ארעא
וצביאת מרת /... בתולתא דא והות ליה לאנתו
ודן נדוניא דהנעלת ליה מבי ... בין בכסף בין בזהב
בשימושא דירה בשימושא דערסא הכל קבל עליו
מו'ה /... חתן דנן במאה זקוקים נסף צרוך וצבי
מו'ה /... חתן דנן והוסיף לה מן דיליה עוד מאה
זקוקים נסף צרוך אחרים כנגדן סך הכל מאתים זקוקים
נסף צרוך וכך אמר מו'ה /... חתן דנן אחריות ישטר
כתובתא דא נדוניא דן ותוספתא דא קבלית עלי ועל
ירתי בתראי להתפרע מנל נפר ארל נכסין וקנינין דאית
ליתחות כל שמיא דקנאי ודעתיד אנא למקנא נכסין דאית
להון אחריות ודלית להון אחריות כלהון יהון אחראין וערבאין
לפרוע מנהון שטר כתובתא דא נדוניא ד... ותוספתא דא
מנאי ואפילו מן גלימא דעל כתפאי בחיי ולבתר חיי מן יומא
דנן ולעלם ואחריות שטר כתובתא דא נדוניא
ותוספתא דא קבל עליו מו'ה /... חתן דנן כחומר
כל שטרי כתובות ותוספות דנהיגין בבנת ישראל
העשויין כתקון חז"ל דלא כאסמכתא ודלא כטופסי
דשטרי וקנינא מן מו'ה /... ... במו'ה ...
חתן דנן למרת /... בת מו'ה ... בתולתא דא
על כלהא דנתוב ומפורש לעיל במנא דכשר למקניאבה
והכל בריר וקיים

נאום ...
ונאום ...

1435 ST. ALEXANDER STREET
SUITE 615

SALES TAX EXTRA

York Fur Inc.

MANUFACTURERS OF FINE FURS

Montreal, Que. H3A 2G4 _____ 197___

Shipped To: _____

Address _____

City _____

| DATE |
| DEPT. No. |
| OUR ORDER No. |
| YOUR ORDER No. |
| TERMS |
| VIA |

STOCK No.	STYLE	QTY.	DESCRIPTION	PRICE	TOTAL
		4			
		1			
		1			
		2			
		4/3			
		4			

NO CLAIMS ALLOWED AFTER 5 DAYS FROM RECEIPT OF GOODS

SHIPPING MEMO

No 3958

From Mrs. Ray Jaskolka

Hamantaschen

4 eggs
1 cup oil
1 cup sugar
2 baking powder
3/4 frozen oranges (juice)
4 cups flour

My parents and me, Pocking DP Camp, American Occupation Zone, Germany, 1947

Determined to begin life again, my parents left the Soviet Union to return to Poland, but with their homes confiscated by their neighbours, and threatened by these usurpers with harm or death, they decided to continue on towards the West. They finally arrived in a displaced persons (refugee) camp in the Occupied American Zone of Germany, in the town of Pocking, which was where I was born exactly 9 months after their wedding night. The families they had left behind were lost in the *Shoah*. My mother lost one brother and his family to the death camps, another brother to typhus during the war. My father lost almost everyone he had known in his *shtetl*: parents, brothers, sisters, nephews, nieces, aunts and uncles.

Pocking DP Camp 1st get-together of survivors in 1948

My father is in the 1st row, far left

My mother's sister, Haya Leah, her husband, Moishe, and their 2 grown children, Pesach and Liebele, in Israel, ca.1960s.

While in Pocking, agents of the Jewish Agency were recruiting Jews to come to Palestine, then ruled by the British, under a mandate conferred to them by the League of Nations after the First World War. My mother wanted to join with her older sister, Haya Leah, and a brother, Zurach Moishe, to emigrate to the new Jewish state, Israel, but my father resisted moving there. He had already seen enough of war and felt that the new Jewish land would soon see more.

In the end, we were sponsored by an uncle in Saint John, New Brunswick. Trained as a tailor, he was ready to fill the demand for this profession in Canada. And so my family and I were transported by ship, the *Nea Hellas*, out of Genoa, Italy, and passed through Pier 21 in Halifax in July, 1948.

ORT tailor training in Pocking DP Camp ca.1947
Note the Yiddish sign in the background

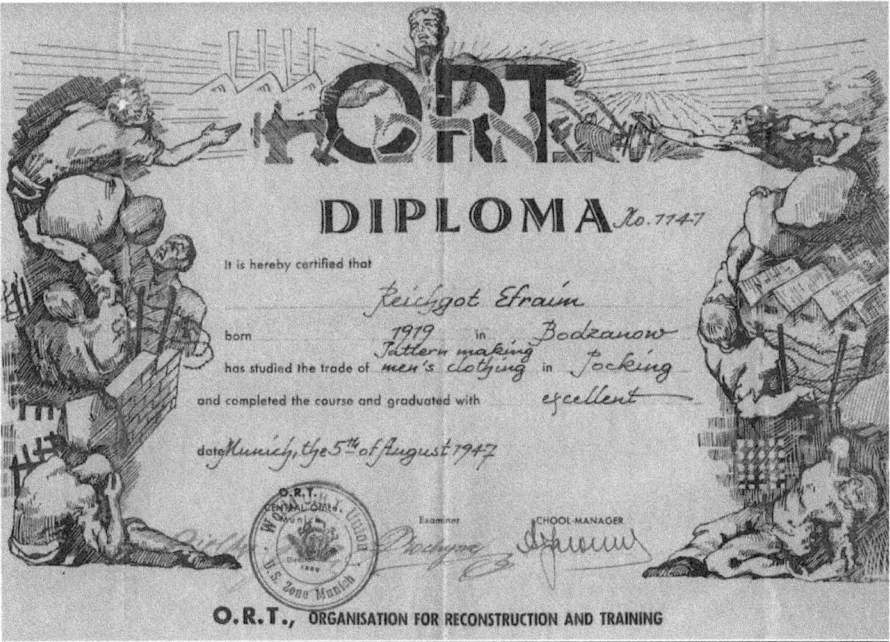

ORT

DIPLOMA No. 1147

It is hereby certified that

Teichgot Efraim

born *1919* in *Bodzanow*

has studied the trade of *men's clothing* in *Pocking*

Tittern making

and completed the course and graduated with *excellent*

date *Munich, the 5th of August 1947*

O.R.T. CENTRAL OFFICE, Munich
U.S. Zone Munich

Examiner

SCHOOL MANAGER

O.R.T., ORGANISATION FOR RECONSTRUCTION AND TRAINING

My father's ORT certificate of training as a tailor in Pocking Camp, Germany

1435 ST. ALEXANDER STREET
SUITE 615

SALES TAX EXTRA

York Fur Inc.

MANUFACTURERS OF FINE FURS

Montreal, Que. H3A 2G4 _____ .197___

DATE

DEPT. No.

OUR ORDER No.

YOUR ORDER No.

Shipped To: _____

Address _____

City _____

TERMS

VIA

STOCK No.	STYLE	QTY.	DESCRIPTION	PRICE	TOTAL

NO CLAIMS ALLOWED AFTER 5 DAYS FROM RECEIPT OF GOODS

SHIPPING MEMO

Nọ 3954

Honey cake

From Mania Steinberg

    1 pint honey
    3 eggs
    1 cup sugar
    3/4 cup oil
    3/4 cup coffee
    1 ground apple
    3 1/2 cups flour
    2 spoons baking powder
    1 spoon baking soda
    Put in nuts

    Oven at 350°, bake for 1 hour.

77 High Street, Saint John, New Brunswick, ca. 1950

After living in Saint John for three years, where my brother Percy was born, it became evident that opportunities were greater in the "*shmatte*" trade in Montreal, and so, once again, we moved, just in time for kindergarten. Montreal had by then welcomed, if that's the right word, more of Europe's Jewish survivors than most other cities in the world. The four of us lived for a year in a rented single bedroom in an apartment on Fairmount Avenue, and I attended Fairmount School. We soon moved to a flat on Esplanade across from Fletcher's Field (now known as Parc Jeanne Mance,) and my brother and I spent the next few years attending Bancroft School on St. Urbain Street. Until I went to school, we all spoke only Yiddish in our home, until one day, when I was in grade 1, I came home from school and boldly declared to my mother that from then on I wasn't going to speak Yiddish any more, only English. I had become a rebel at age 6. And that was how my parents learned most of their English—from me and my brother.

Gefilte fish

TEL.: 844-3397
844-3398

1435 ST. ALEXANDER STREET
SUITE 615

York Fur Inc.

MANUFACTURERS OF FINE FURS

Montreal, Que. H3A 2G4 _____ 197___

Shipped To: _____

Address _____

City _____

SALES TAX EXTRA

DATE

DEPT. No.

OUR ORDER No.

YOUR ORDER No.

TERMS

VIA

STOCK No.	STYLE	QTY.	DESCRIPTION	PRICE	TOTAL

NO CLAIMS ALLOWED AFTER 5 DAYS FROM RECEIPT OF GOODS

SHIPPING MEMO

№ 3956

Goldie's Kichelech

From Goldie in Kibbutz Eilon, Israel

For kichelech

400 grams margarine
3 eggs
1 and 1/4 glass sugar
1 baking powder
1 spoon oil
5 glasses flour

kichelech from Goldie

All the neighbours on Esplanade Street and the surrounding neighbourhood spoke Yiddish. On Sunday mornings, the day of rest which for many replaced *shabbos*, the men of the neighbourhood would gather at the corner of Park and Mount Royal Avenues, around the stone horse trough, and argue matters of great importance, all in Yiddish–politics, religion, philosophy, and commentary on the news from Canada, The United States, Europe, and of course, Israel, then just a fledgeling state struggling to keep its people fed and protected from harm. This was many years before Israel, after it won the Six Day War by what seemed to all of us a miracle, changed overnight from David to Goliath in the eyes of the rest of the world.

Hundreds of thousands of Jews were arriving in Israel from Europe, and then the forced expulsion of Jews from Arab countries following the the 1956 Sinai War between Israel, Great Britain, and France on one side, and Egypt on the other, brought many more immigrants to Israel. In order to enhance the use of Hebrew as the country's official language, and to unify all these diverse new arrivals, there was a concerted effort in the early days of the fledgling state of Israel to discourage the use and teaching of Yiddish.

Matza ball soup

From Maketo shnapler
Resepy paeech zemt

2 קאפס מאצאה מעל
צאלץ 1 לעפעלעלה
צוקער 1 לעפעלעלה
וואסער 1 קאפ
אויל 1/2 טעפעלעלה
4 אייעקס —

אפקאכן די וואסער
אין אריין טון די מאצאמעל
צאלץ אפקאכן
אין אריין טון די מאצאה מעל
אין דער נאמדעם צו אייעקס
עדוושעלע אויך באזונדער
אין מישן אין לאזן שטיין

Recipe from Malka Schneider

Pesach Rolls (zemel)

2 cups matzo meal
1 teaspoon salt
1 teaspoon sugar
1 cup water
1/2 pot oil
4 eggs

Boil the water and add the matzo meal
let it cool
and add the matzo meal (?)
mix in the 4 eggs, adding in each egg by itself at a time
mix together and lay flat

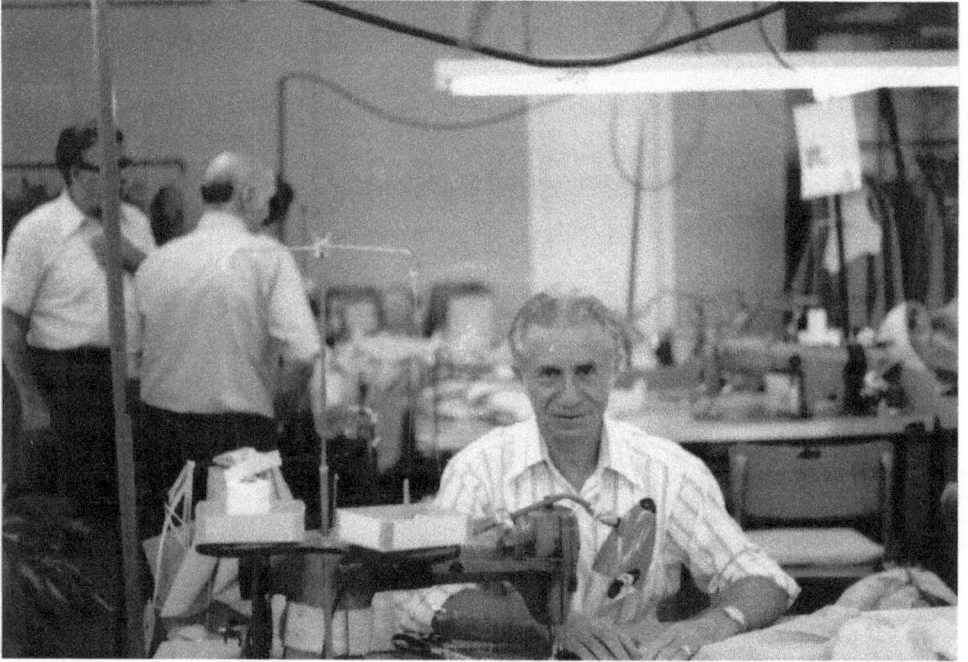

My father at work at his sewing machine job

For a time, St Lawrence Boulevard remained the centre of the "*shmatte* trade," the textile manufacturing factories that produced much of Canada's clothing. Unions were becoming stronger, but sweatshops were still the rule, not the exception.

My father was a sewing machine operator in the downtown garment district around lower St. Lawrence Street, working in women's clothing, and was a member of ILGWU, the International Ladies Garment Workers Union.

1435 ST. ALEXANDER STREET
SUITE 615

SALES TAX EXTRA

York Fur Inc.

MANUFACTURERS OF FINE FURS

Montreal, Que. H3A 2G4 _____ 197____

Shipped To: _____ [Hebrew handwriting] רעכאב: בן בן אהרן שלרן' אויע
Address
City _____ 448- 1678 _____ [Hebrew] אברהם בן

DATE	
DEPT. No.	
OUR ORDER No.	
YOUR ORDER No.	
TERMS	
VIA	

STOCK No.	STYLE	QTY.	DESCRIPTION	PRICE	TOTAL
			3 חלקים [Hebrew]	[Hebrew] אוק אבא:זלץ	
			3 שוועבער [Hebrew]	8½ שלעק	
			1 קלף 3.קרן	נ"ע מליק	
			1 קלף 8½		
			3 קנים 2 קלאב/3		
			2 שוועבער חלקים		
			3/4 קרוב מעויל		
חלקים	סעכס 8 [Hebrew]		[Hebrew handwriting]		

NO CLAIMS ALLOWED AFTER 5 DAYS FROM RECEIPT OF GOODS

SHIPPING MEMO

Nº 3952

44

Mandel broit

Recipe from Mrs. Goldberg

3 eggs
3 cups meal
1 cup sugar
3 baking powder
2 spoons almonds?
3/4 quarter almonds
If desired, you can add more almond spice

When baked, cut into slices, and in the night burn.

The Plateau Mount Royal was then a lower working class neighbourhood with slum-like conditions, not the gentrified area we know now. It was home to countless once-impoverished Jewish refugee families who had fled Europe after the war, and many were beginning to succeed and move on to better parts of the city.

Apartments were poorly heated and poorly maintained, paint and plaster peeling, with mice in the walls and silverfish in the drains and on the floors, but schools were of high quality. Fairmount Elementary, Bancroft Elementary (which I attended) and Baron Byng High (which I didn't attend because we had moved away when I was 10), were excellent, and started many young Jews on the road to successful professional careers in teaching, research, the health fields, accounting, business,and law. These schools were part of the Protestant School Board of Greater Montreal, and were primarily English-speaking. Because we were Jewish, by the rules of that time we were not eligible to attend the Catholic-run schools, which were primarily French-speaking. And so we grew up attached to the English language, not to that of the French majority. My Yiddish languished. It was time to prepare for my bar mitzvah, so I learned to read the Torah portion and the required prayers in Hebrew. Yiddish remained off to the side somewhere, largely erased from my memory.

Hamantaschen

On top of all her other duties of keeping a clean and kosher house, shopping, cooking, washing up, and making sure her sons were encouraged in their school work, my mother helped with the family finances, this despite my father's opposition to her taking a job. It was a more traditional time, and women were expected to be housewives only, not work outside the home. At the same time, my father worked very hard at his factory job during the day, and took in extra work from contractors at home in the evenings and on weekends.

My mother's independent spirit had been hardened because of the time she spent in a Soviet labour camp during the war years, and the harsh conditions she endured in war-time Russia. My mother knew hard work and wasn't afraid of it. Once my brother started school, and despite my father's protests, she went to work sewing fur coats in a clandestine factory shop close to our flat. After a few years, my parents had accumulated a few dollars, and we moved to a half-duplex my father bought in Notre Dame de Grace (NDG), in the western part of Montreal.

פין פפר פאנטינרטשל

489-6152

הב"א צאזר

4   אליקס

1/2   אליסר

אזלר ם לצראעד אליקן   6588

1/4   אליערן

1   קהל אליבים אליבים אימ

4   אימ נ' 13 אליסר

אימ ל' 3 אלק אין 3. צלם

אלק 13 אליסר

אלק 383 לקהנ3

16 אלק אלקין 3. אלקר

אלק אין 3 10 צאלד אלקים

צלד אלקר אלק לי אלק אלק

פינאצאר

From Pearl Blumenkrantz

Matzo balls recipe

4 eggs
1/2 cup water
a small spoon of salt
1/4 margarine
1 cup matzo meal
Mix in the water with the eggs and salt
Next add the matzo meal
Let stand for 1 hour in the refrigerator

My parents, Frank and Ester Rajchgot, and my brother Percy, in my mother's kitchen in NDG, ca. 1970

Passover cake

From Mrs. Goldman

9 eggs: separate the yolks, to the egg yolks, add 1 glass sugar
2 glasses ground nuts
1/2 lemon ground with the rest
1 glass cake meal
with 3 spoons sugar

Next, mix together the eggs yolks with the egg whites
Set the oven at 300°
Let the cake stand 1/2 hour in the oven, then raise the temperature
to 350° for 1 hour

My mother was only able to attend school to the third grade in Poland. Her spelling skills in Yiddish were poor, and yet she maintained a correspondence in that language with her family members in Israel and in other parts of North America. Communication was almost exclusively by mail then. Long distance telephone calls were too expensive, and were kept as short as possible, used only for very important matters, like severe illness, death, or family occasions—bar mitzvahs and marriages. I still have a number of my mother's letters received from her sister and her niece in Israel. All these were of course written by women, and to women. Men were not letter writers. They had more important things to do- livings to earn, synagogues and meetings to attend. They had little to do with raising their children, transmitting their stories, or preparing the home for the holidays. So in the home, women were the carriers of culture, religious practice, and, of course, the feeding of their husbands and children. They bought the ingredients for cooking, prepared and cooked the food, carried it from stovetop and oven to table, and cleaned up afterwards. It was they who were involved with nutrition, taste, *kashrut,* and the repertoire of foods which were appropriate to feed their families at the various Jewish holidays and festivals. They knew which flavours would please their husband's palates, and how much food could be heaped on a child's plate to make sure that he didn't starve to death or suffer from the constant threat (in their minds) of malnutrition. They had brought their memories of food insecurity from before the war and especially during it, and made sure their children never suffered a hungry moment. Seeing a child eat was a source of great comfort. Seeing a child reject food created anxiety and a feeling of inadequacy. Guilt and anxiety, those great motivators of Jewish life in the past, lived on in them, and centred on their children, and were passed on to them and the next generation of these children's children in turn.

Ess,ess, mein kint!

Despite all the difficulties of living through the War, losing family and home, and moving and adjusting to a new country, my parents and their generation knew how to live. They celebrated whenever there was any reason to do so, whether a bar mitzvah, a wedding, or when the Jewish holidays brought them together, or simply if it happened to be a nice day. They were members of Jewish groups, like the *Arbeiter Ring*, and loved ballroom dancing and sharing a *schnapps,* or listening to a musical performance around the bandstand on the eastern slopes of Mount Royal (which was recently named, with the usual local controversy, after the late, renowned Montreal writer, Mordecai Richler, who lived in the area.) On many Sundays, families gathered at home for a festive dinner, which is what they called the midday meal, like the good British cultural citizens they had become, serving up a seemingly endless array of appetizers, soups, main courses, and desserts. Life was to be lived, and mourning was restricted to *yuhrzeits* and Yom Kippur. The future was where they were heading, the past was something to leave behind as much as was possible. They had growing families, and this was where their concerns were concentrated.

In 1958, we moved from the Plateau to NDG. The kitchen was larger and more functional, and my mother would cook some of the week's meals on the weekend, while my father took in extra work from contractors, working at home on his own industrial sewing machine. My mother continued to work downtown in a fur factory, but somehow managed to maintain a clean home, and a busy kitchen, while my brother and I lazed around, oblivious to the hard work of my parents, but excelling in school, first high school, at Monklands High on West Hill Avenue, and later at McGill University.

Social gathering among friends and acquaintances

When I began the translation of these recipes, over 70 in all, I had trouble with deciphering them. The Yiddish cursive writing that my mother used to record them was difficult to read. Besides the difficulty with her handwriting, there was also the unusual phonetic spellings of words. The mix of English transliterated into Yiddish letters made it even harder to work out at times. This was definitely not what is known as Standard Yiddish. For example, adapting a word like **"orange juice"** to a mix of Hebrew letters took some figuring out.

And then there was the matter of the units my mother used in her measurements. A t*eppele* was not the same as a *teppel.* The one was a cup, and the other was a–I don't know really–maybe a small cup. A *leffel* was a tablespoon, I think, a *leffeleh,* a teaspoon. And in some recipes, the units aren't mentioned at all, and one has to use some insight to know the context, that "one milk" would be a cup of milk, and one sugar could be a teaspoon, a tablespoon, or even a cup. It was all a matter of proportion. In some cases, I could use the number of eggs in a recipe to figure out what units the other ingredients were measured in. Something like a Rosetta Stone for cooks instead of linguists. I was groping in the dark.

There were also many iterations of the same recipe, sourced from different women, which had probably made a circle from one to the next and back around. Broken telephone for cooks. I was surprised, once I had started to translate them, that most of these shared recipes were for cakes and cookies, some for everyday, and others for Passover. My mother didn't use recorded recipes for her own cooking. The instructions for most of the food she cooked sat in in her head and, sadly, were never written down, and are therefore now lost. There were certain things, such as bread eaten throughout the week, that was store-bought—my mother never baked bread, although she did bake passover matzah rolls, which were much tastier than plain matzah. At the time, matzah came in 2 varieties, plain (kosher for Passover) and egg (not kosher for Passover), which tasted better, especially after the first few days of plain. Not much of a choice.

My mother prepared lunches for my father to take to work, and school lunches for me, and for my younger brother. I brought a salami sandwich to school pretty much every day—salami on rye bread—with an apple or a banana. Fresh bread was imperative, at my father's insistence, a reminder that once, during the war years, it had been unattainable. Now it had the special value of something once lost and miraculously found again.

From Makto shnapder
Resepy paeech zemt

---

2 קאפס מאצאלה מויל
זאלץ 1 לעפעלעלה
צוקער 1 לעפעלעלה
וואסער 1 קאפ
אויל 1/2 טעפעלעלה
4 אוועקס —

אפקאכן די וואסער
אין אריין טון די מאצאמויל
זאלץ אפקילן
און אריין טון די מאצאלה מויל
און דער נאכדעם די אוועקס
יעדעס עפּעלע אויף באקינגער
אין אויוון און לאזן שטיין

Recipe from Malka Schneider
Pesach Rolls (zemel)

2 cups matzo meal
1 teaspoon salt
1 teaspoon sugar
1 cup water
1/2 pot oil
4 eggs

Boil the water and add the matzo meal
let it cool
and add the matzo meal (?)
4 eggs in the noodle (?) adding 1 egg by itself at a time
mix together and lay flat

or:

4 eggs
1 spoon sugar
1 spoon salt
1/2 oil
1 cup water
2 pots matzo meal

Boil the water
Add salt
Add oil
Let the eggs cook
You have to beat them together
When it cools off, add eggs
Leave the second part
Don't mix all of it together
Let stand in the refrigerator for 1 hour

When I was a child in Montreal, I don't recall my mother talking about the quality of food in the DP camp where I was born, likely because there wasn't much of it. It was in the town of Pocking, in the American Zone of Occupation. What she did say had to do with the hunger and the lack of food. What she did remember, and made her laugh, were the the loaves of bread handed out by the U.S. Army when she and my father first arrived there—pure white, and, my mother marveled, it never got stale. It could become mouldy and still appear soft and fresh-looking. It was a wonder, she said. Maybe the white sliced bread still found on the supermarket shelves today was called *Wonder Bread* for that reason. The preference in our home, though, was for European-style breads, crusty, heavy and chewy, bought at the local bakeries, the Arena Bakery at the corner of Mount Royal and Saint Urban streets, or the Saint Lawrence Bakery on the Main, near the corner of Rachel (both are gone now). The Warshaw food store on Saint Lawrence (also gone now) was where she bought many of her fruits and vegetables. The selection of these was very limited compared to today's cornucopia—whatever was being harvested at the time, or could be stored through winter or transported from the southern U.S and its banana republics to its south, like, of course, bananas, and many citrus fruits.

אורז 12

קמח אלף 1½

בסולת אלף בסולת ½

שמן 1½ בסולת אלף

½ בסולת אורז בסולת

Unknown recipe with unnamed source

Pesach (Passover) plate

TEL.: 844-3397
844-3398

1435 ST. ALEXANDER STREET
SUITE 615

York Fur Inc.

MANUFACTURERS OF FINE FURS

Montreal, Que. H3A 2G4 _____ 197____

Shipped To: _____

Address _____

City _____

			SALES TAX EXTRA
DATE			
DEPT. No.			
OUR ORDER No.			
YOUR ORDER No.			
TERMS			
VIA			

STOCK No.	STYLE	QTY.	DESCRIPTION	PRICE	TOTAL

NO CLAIMS ALLOWED AFTER 5 DAYS FROM RECEIPT OF GOODS

SHIPPING MEMO

Nº 3959

64

Regina Kornfeld

Potato knishes

3 eggs
3 grated poatoes
Fry together
Add in onion with a little oil
A little spice
Put in with a spoon in a baking pan

I remember my mother's cooking. She was a good cook, but when I was young, I didn't much appreciate it. It was everyday cooking to me, my mother's repertoire of dishes—roast chicken, meat loaf, brisket, and chicken soup seeming nothing special, and it was only as an adult that I came to appreciate its special flavours. The chicken my mother used came from the kosher *shoihet* or butcher at the Rachel Street market. I would come with her as she did her shopping, choosing the chicken (alive and clucking), having it ritually slaughtered—something I observed with both fascination and revulsion. She would pluck the feathers and burn off the remnant quills still attached to the skin there at the butcher's shop at a gas burner poking through one wall, then bring the dead bird home and chop it into sections with a meat cleaver on a wooden chopping board. The pieces sat immersed in an enameled iron bucket of cold water and were sprinkled with kosher salt, according to the demands of *kashrut*. There they sat for a time—an hour, a few hours—I don't really remember—so that the blood would be drawn out of the meat into the water This was the koshering process, hence the term kosher salt, and the meat would then be suitable for cooking and eating in a Jewish home.

My mother did all of the mixing, grinding, mashing, squeezing, and chopping by herself, by hand. She didn't have a food processor, a blender, or an electric mixer. The microwave oven was not yet on the horizon, and the stove used gas, not electricity. When we spent a few weeks in Val Morin or Prevost in the Laurentians with her and another family, the stove burned wood. We picked blueberries in clearings in the woods, coming back with baskets of them. My mother baked blueberry pies and pastries with these, along with the regular cooking of meals, especially for Friday night's *shabbos* meal, when her husband would arrive famished from the city. My father would take a bus up and spend the weekend before returning to work. The house we rented belonged to a poor Québecois farm family, who vacated it for the summer to earn a few needed dollars, and spent the summer living in a smaller, more cramped cottage close-by.

These weeks away were a luxury, but something my father considered important. He wanted his sons to breathe fresh country air, get some sunshine, and learn a little bit about the natural world that was so remote and exotic for residents of the inner city.

All the red meat we ate (beef, or rarely, veal) was bought at a butcher shop off a back alley in the Plateau area. While she was in the butcher shop, my mother usually left me in the laneway while she went in to buy her meat. One particular time at the butcher shop gave me my fear of dogs, when one, a very large one, which seemed 7 or 8 feet tall but of course wasn't, began barking fiercely at me (I must have been about 7 or 8 years old at the time, so one dog-foot per year) while she was inside making her meat purchase. My mother rushed outside to rescue me. I never forgot the image of this large black dog jumping around me, yelping at me, and I'm still wary of dogs, especially the large ones.

There was no helicopter parenting then—children were left on their own outside for hours at a time except when the weather turned bad. We came home from school before our parents arrived from work, let ourselves in with our own key, and spent the period before their arrival doing our homework. I never heard of any one of us coming to any harm because of this.

It was a different time.

DRY

2 PKGS EAST

4 CUPS FLOUR

2 EGGS

PINCH OF SALT

2 SCAPS SUGAR

½ PKG OF CRISCO

COVER AND LET RISE

TO DOUBLE THE SIZE

881 1121

Pie crust

Recipe from Leah in Toronto

2 packages dry yeast
4 cups flour
2 eggs
pinch of salt
2 cups (scaps?) sugar
1/2 pkg crisco

Cover and let rise to double size. Roll over and then lay flat and roll again

The kitchen was always busy—we were two growing boys and my father was always hungry when he got home from work. My mother cooked and baked her own gefilte fish. She made her own blintzes, kreplach, latkes, egg noodles, and matzoh brei, as the holidays came and went, plus she cooked all the main courses, too. There was no dishwasher or microwave oven, and the men of the house rarely pitched in. Sorry, Mom, looking back now, for not helping.

There weren't many herbs or spices in my mother's cooking. Salt and pepper, of course, garlic, onion, and celery, and, rarely, paprika or dill gave flavour to her food, but my mother did make a mean brisket or roast chicken for special occasions.

Over the years, the strictness of *kashrut* in my mother's kitchen relaxed. After we moved to the Notre Dame de Grace (NDG) district of Montreal, she bought her meat at Steinberg's supermarket (which later went bankrupt, so it no longer exists), and cooked it without the intervening ritual treatment in the bucket. The taste got better accordingly, maybe, although the broth was perhaps less palatable for my father. It was about then that I first tasted a Jaffa orange, a new import from Israel. We were eager to buy these, since we were supporting the agricultural kibbutzim by doing so. They were delicious. What ever happened to them?

My father's tomato plants

For his part, my father made his own sour (dill) pickles, growing dill in a patch of ground in the backyard or next to the driveway of our house in NDG, buying warty cucumbers and pickling spices, garlic, and coarse kosher salt at the market, and leaving it all to ferment in large jars on a shelf in the garage for a week or two. He also grew tomatoes, which became ripe just as the local farmers' crop arrived at the supermarket.

Since then, I've always tried to keep up the tradition by growing a few herbs and vegetables in my own back yard garden. I don't remember so many aggressive squirrels, groundhogs, skunks, and raccoons back then, though.

Jewish food has been linked in many ways to the Jewish calendar, the cycle of holidays. It was also deeply affected by the laws concerning food found in the Book of Leviticus in the Torah (The Five Books of Moses). These laws determined whether a particular food was kosher or not—it had to pass through a series of tests. Permitted were cloven hooves and cud-chewing for domestic mammals, fins and scales for sea creatures, whether they were predators or not for birds of the air, and some arcane categories, no longer used, such as the permissibility of certain locusts.

For plants, there were rules for their farming and harvesting, such as leaving the corners of the fields unharvested, and allowing the land to remain fallow every seven years (where the term sabbatical came from.) Certain plants could not be used because insects might lodge in the spaces between their leaves and florets. Milk products had their own sets of rules. The permissibility of meat, poultry, and fish were controlled by its methods of slaughtering, and by its preparation, as set out in commentaries on the rules in later books, such as in the Talmud. Some foods, even if allowed, could not be eaten with certain other foods, such as milk and meat. On Passover, there was a ban on leavened bread, and any other grain product that hadn't been processed in a restrictive manner. There were two sets of dishes, one for milk and another for meat, and for Passover two separate sets that were not used during the rest of the year. Dishware, cookware and utensils were strictly controlled. There were rules for everything, rules upon rules, just in case, by some omission, something unacceptable might get by. And it was this strict adherence to the complicated laws of *kashrut* which in many ways kept the Jewish people apart from their neighbours, and so, unable to mingle, they were kept from dwindling away, as happened to many other ancient peoples.

Challahs at an outdoor bakery in Jerusalem.

The weekly Sabbath meal on Friday night became a tradition, with its own traditional foods. The Friday evening meal was prepared during the day on Friday, and was a special meal, more elaborate and with richer and more expensive ingredients. The table was set with a white cloth, and the candles lit.

The meal begins with the blessings over the wine and bread. The bread was *challah*, an egg bread, made with white flour. It was braided and glazed with egg whites, golden and shiny, and this made it not only tasty, but also visually attractive. The *shabbos* meal also often included a chicken soup with egg noodles, boiled chicken with root vegetables such as parsnips, carrots, and potatoes. Alongside this was beet borscht and tsimmes, a sweet carrot dish. Because of the sacredness of the Sabbath, when no fire could be lit and no work (included cutting vegetables) done, the slow-cooking hot pot meal called *cholent* (which my mother called *chunt)* was started before the onset of the Sabbath at sunset on Friday. It bubbled away on low heat all night and all day Saturday. There were also special meals or foods associated with the various holidays throughout the year.

TEL.: 844-3397
844-3398

1435 ST. ALEXANDER STREET
SUITE 615

York Fur Inc.

MANUFACTURERS OF FINE FURS

Montreal, Que. H3A 2G4 _____ ‏ודנוצ‎ 3 197____

Shipped To: _____ Shmaovish   Shevin ‏ןיב‎ ____

Address _____ 488-6456

City _____

	SALES TAX EXTRA	
DATE		
DEPT. No.		
OUR ORDER No.		
YOUR ORDER No.		
TERMS		
VIA		

STOCK No.	STYLE	QTY.	DESCRIPTION	PRICE	TOTAL
	‏קווןס‎	2	‏קווןס 4‎		
	‏3יקרצ‎	1/2	‏פ/ןק פ4סו 1‎		
‏פ/ןק‎	פ4סת	1/2	‏3יקרצ פ/1ס1‎		
	‏פ7קו‎	1/2	‏פ7קו פקס 1‎		
‏קו2/צ‎ ‏צ/יקוצ‎	1		‏פ3כ2פ צ/יקוצ 2‎		
‏פ2/2ק‎ ‏צ/יקוצ‎	1/4		‏פ/צ/2ק צ/יקוצ 1/4‎		
‏סוא‎ ‏צרג"פפ‎	2		‏סוא פסקו 4‎		
‏פ/צףצ פ/ק פ/פ‎					
	‏ודנוצ‎				

NO CLAIMS ALLOWED AFTER 5 DAYS FROM RECEIPT OF GOODS

SHIPPING   MEMO

Nº   3964

From Sharon Shmarish

Honey cake

4 eggs
1 glass honey
1 glass sugar
1 cup coffee
2 baking powder
1/4 baking soda
4 cups flour

Half-recipe:

2 eggs
1/2 sugar
1/2 glass honey
1/2 coffee
1 baking powder
1/4 baking soda
2 glasses flour

In this recipe book, I've included many of the dishes I found among my mother's papers. Many well-known Jewish dishes are not among those included here because my mother never wrote them down, even though she cooked them. She didn't need a written recipe—it was in her head. I can still taste them in my head, their aromas tickling the sense of smell of my imagination.

So, as my mother would say, "*What, you're not eating? You don't like my food?*"

And as my father would say, in Yiddish, "*Hup arein!*" ("Grab it while it's still there!")

So enjoy!

מי מכבד ואבניגלאי

והמסרבי   489-6152

4' אייקים

3/4 אכזב כראו ס/23ס

1/2 שייפנא/(אן)

4 בייחובוג פלאני כאברת

והיכו וביכו וביכו כין כי מכברל

80

From Pearl Rosenblum

Roly Poly

4 eggs
3/4 orange juice
1/2 cup oil
4 baking powder

This is a translation of the beginning of a memoir that my mother began to write in 2002, many years after the war had ended. A little over a year later, her health took a drastic change for the worse, and she was never able to write anything more about her past.

This Is What We Lived Through

by Ester Rajchgot

In 1939, the war began. We were forced to rush away from our homes. We wandered from one place to another place. The Germans chased us and we ran. We had my sister's 2 small children with us, one child who was 3 months old and the other was 1½ years old. It was very hard, but it was even more difficult for the children. My sister had no way to give them something to eat. She had no milk for them The Germans didn't let us take any diapers for the children with us. It was very hard for us. The Germans chased us to the Russian border. We crossed that border and were saved.

Yiddish as History

This may be an obvious statement, but food has always been an important part of being Jewish. Since the 613 Commandments were handed down to Moses at Mount Sinai, eating kosher has been a central part of the Jewish identity, and may be one of the most important reasons Jews remained culturally, socially, ethnically, and religiously separate from their gentile neighbours over the thousands of years following their expulsion from Israel by the Romans in 135 C.E.

Many were taken as slaves to Rome and the many provinces of its empire. They were forbidden from entering Jerusalem and what the Romans began to call Palestine once the Jews were gone. These diaspora Jews were soon competing with the offshoot religion of Christianity and later with Islam, and were forced to migrate again and again, with large groups settling in Iberia, (later to become Spain amd Portugal), Italy, then France and Germany, and later in Poland and the Russian Pale of Settlement. Many ended up in the Ottoman (Turkish) Empire and North Africa. Many still remained in what was once Babylon (now Iraq), so Jews lived everywhere in the known world. And wherever Jews travelled,as traders, not tourists, they could find local Jews and could communicate using one or other of the languages that Jews developed in these places.

Over time, Yiddish developed, as did many other Hebrew-derived languages, such as Ladino. In the Germanic territories, the Hebrew language blended with the German tongue to form Yiddish, which became the vernacular for the millions of Jews who lived in Eastern Europe for many centuries, before the Holocaust almost destroyed them all.

For these Yiddish-speaking wandering Jews, some times were good, some times were not so good, and some times were terrible, as famine and pestilence, pogroms and war, came and went across wide swaths of Eastern Europe from the 1700s through the late 1800s. Once again, antisemitic turmoil propelled Jews away from the lands they had inhabited for a thousand years. Many fled the Russian Empire in the late 1800s, because of expulsions and restrictions on places of domicile and occupations they were permitted to have. Poverty and oppression were major factors pushing Jews to move on. Young Jewish men were routinely conscripted into the Czar's army for periods of 25 years before regaining their freedom. Jews who could find a way to do so left for a better life in Canada and the United States in the late 1800s and onward, until the 1920s and 1930s, when immigration restrictions started being imposed.

In the last century, as we know too well, conditions in Germany became increasingly harsh after the accession to power in Germany by Hitler's Nazis. The attempt to flee Germany before the start of the war was cruelly restricted by the German government, and reduced to a trickle at the receiving end by Canada and most other countries around the world. Some who tried to leave by ship were forced to return in these ships that had brought them from Germany, and many of them later died in concentration camps, forced labour camps, and extermination camps. Most could not even try to escape. They remained behind, and when the German invasion of Poland and then most of the rest of Europe came, Nazi hatred culminated in the Holocaust. The Jewish population of Europe was decimated and this brought an end to *shtetl* life and much of the culture of Eastern European Jewry. Many Jews ended up in displaced persons (refugee) camps after the war ended. This included my parents.

1435 ST. ALEXANDER STREET
SUITE 615

SALES TAX EXTRA

York Fur Inc.

MANUFACTURERS OF FINE FURS

Montreal, Que. H3A 2G4 _____ שבט _____ 197__

Shipped To: _____ ציאקסאן פור אילעריש ל_____

Address _____

City _____

484-4104

DATE
DEPT. No.
OUR ORDER No.
YOUR ORDER No.
TERMS
VIA

STOCK No.	STYLE	QTY.	DESCRIPTION	PRICE	TOTAL

NO CLAIMS ALLOWED AFTER 5 DAYS FROM RECEIPT OF GOODS

SHIPPING MEMO

Nº 3966

Recipe from Malkeleh Schneider

Kugel (kiggel)

3 eggs
3 matzos
apple
3/4 sugar
raisins
1/4 lemon juice
mix it all together

4 eggs in the noodle (?) adding 1 egg by itself at a time
mix together and lay flat

Once the war was over, there was a sudden influx of Jewish immigrants to North America and Israel, along with other countries around the world, where Jews could feel safe and were welcomed. Among these refugees were my parents and me. These Jews brought Yiddish with them, but soon the need to integrate put pressure on the use of Yiddish, especially in the generations which succeeded them, specifically, my brother and me. To make friends, be accepted by our peers—be they Jewish or not—get by in school as Canadians, not as foreigners, find jobs, or positions—in other words, so we could make a living, make a success of ourselves, start our own families and our own businesses, build our reputations—these all meant that Yiddish would be left behind. We wanted to be like everyone else, not foreigners, not to feel the otherness that my parents had lived in the old country.

Hebrew was the common language of the Jews from about 1000 BCE until the destruction of the First Temple by the Babylonians. It is the language that the Five Books of Moses (The Torah), The Prophets (Nevi'im), and The Writings (Ketuvim), together known as the Tanach—the Hebrew Bible—are written in, and it is still used as the language of Jewish prayer. The Assyrian destruction and exile of the Kingdom of Israel left only the Kingdom of Judah intact. There the language of everyday usage became Aramaic, a variant of Hebrew. With the destruction of the Second Temple (70 CE), and the expulsion of the Jews from their land by the Romans (135 CE), Hebrew became restricted to mainly liturgical uses, although most Jews could read and understand it because it was part of their daily prayers and the basis of their legal code. Only in the late 19th and in the 20th Century was Modern Hebrew revived as a spoken vernacular language, and it became the official language of the State of Israel in 1948, where it is once again a living language.

After the Jewish revolts, the Romans renamed the area Palestina, after the Philistines, the ancient enemies of the Jews of King David's time. The Jews were dispersed within the Roman Empire, many as slaves. Persia still retained a residual population of Jews remaining there after the Persian conquest hundreds of years earlier.

Exiles combined their Aramaic and Hebrew with local languages, and new Jewish languages evolved. Hebrew was restricted for use in the synagogue. These evolving tongues used the Hebrew alphabet in their written form. One of the best-known of these languages is Yiddish, which derived much of its vocabulary by contact with German dialects. It was the *mame-loshen,* or mother tongue of the Jews of Eastern Europe, as opposed to the *loshen koydesh*, the holy tongue, as Hebrew was referred to. At its height, before the Second World War, Yiddish was used in everyday speech by some 11-13 million Yiddish speakers, of about 17 million Jews world-wide at the time. When the Holocaust devastated Jewish communities, Yiddish was nearly destroyed as a living language. 85% of the 6 million Jews who died in the Holocaust were Yiddish speakers, many without a name.

Nudlman.   פ.ר א.וו.סוו

486-8316

From Mrs. Nudelman

Recipe with no name

3 egg whites
a pinch of salt
1/2 cup sugar
1 spoon potato starch
1 teaspoon lemon juice

Yiddish was initially discouraged in the early days after the founding of the State of Israel, in order to shore up the use of Hebrew among the many new arrivals from Europe who probably would have preferred to speak it. At the time, it was considered the language of shame, the language of oppression, by Israelis, and its use was repressed. Yiddish is gaining speakers there now, though. For some, it is being learned because of a sentimental longing for the past and the language's roots among the European Jews who arrived in Israel before and after World War II. It is still used today as the largely exclusive language of daily interaction among many of the *haredi* Jews living both in Israel and the Diaspora, for whom Hebrew is the holy tongue, to be used only in prayer.

In North America, Yiddish is making a resurgence too, attracting not only Jews but non-Jews as well. It is the language of writers such as Sholom Aleichem, Isaac Bashevis Singer, and Elie Wiesel. It lives on in the lyrics of many klezmer songs, and has become part of the vernacular of English in North America.

Here in Montreal, Hirsch Wolofsky founded the Yiddish newspaper *Keneder Adler* (Canadian Eagle) in 1907. The Yiddish poets Sholom Shtern and Chava Rosenfarb, among many others, wrote here. The Dora Wasserman Yiddish Theatre was founded by Dora Wasserman, a Holocaust survivor and acquaintance of my mother, and it is still a vibrant part of the Montreal Jewish community, performing at the Segal Centre. The Montreal writer Norm Ravvin is the author of, among others, a book of short stories titled *Sex, Skyscrapers, and Standard Yiddish*. The sitcom *YidLife Crisis*, is a comic take on the foibles of a group of Jewish young people here in Montreal, and is performed entirely in Yiddish. Klezmer groups and musicians, such as *The Bagg Street Klezmer Band, Shtreiml, Magillah, Mazik, The Black Ox Orkestar, Kleztory, Siach Hasadeh*, and even an all-Québecois band, *Octopus*, have sprung up playing variations of traditional Eastern European tunes, often with Yiddish lyrics, and the annual KlezKanada camp meets every year in August on the grounds of the B'nai Brith summer camp in the Laurentians north of Montreal, and it fosters the growth of this art form in Canada and across North America. Yiddish is alive and well, and growing by the day.

I grew up surrounded by Yiddish. It was my mother tongue and the air I breathed. The Mile End and Plateau neighbourhoods of Montreal, where my family lived in the 1950s before moving to NDG (Notre Dame de Grace), had been a Jewish area since the early years of the 20th Century. It was natural, then, that it would be the first landing place of many of the Jews newly-arrived from Europe after WWII, having seen their generation, their families, towns, villages, synagogues, community centres, and their culture and language almost destroyed by Hitler's killing machine. These survivors rebuilt their lives here, in many cases trying to leave behind their Jewish and Yiddish heritage, or if not them, then their children did, while trying to integrate into their new land. As part of that shucking of heritage, as I mentioned, I was a part—I came home from school one day at the age of 6 and declared to my mother that I would no longer speak to her in Yiddish, and it was only much later, when I visited Israel, that I tried to dredge up my memories of Yiddish so that I could converse with my relatives there. And there it sat, a sad relic for many years, largely untouched, until, as I grew older, I came to understand its attraction and power. Now many are embarking on the study of Yiddish again, delighted by its beauty and its earthiness, its *menchlichkeit*, its *tum*. And thus, this book is the result, speaking of the past and the power and tenacity of women, of food and its delights, of the rope of wisdom and culture which connects us to our past, and makes us whole, and binds us together as we rise into our unseen future.

אָ אַ ב בֿ בּ ג ד ה ו וּ וו וי ז ח ט י יִ יי ײַ כ כּ ך ל מ ם נ ן ס ע פ פּ פֿ ף צ ץ ק ר ש שׂ ת תּ

Acknowledgements

I wish to thank the Foundation for Yiddish Culture for their financial support. Thanks are also due to Sivan Slapak for convincing me to put this material in writing, and so preserve my mother's legacy. I dedicate this book to my late mother, Ester Rajchgot, who taught me how and what to eat, and how and when to speak (not just in Yiddish) plus other important things. Her life inspired the writing of this book. Her food nourished me and my family over much of my lifetime, so this is a tribute to her, her love of family, her love of life, her determination, good sense, courage, and hard work.

I also wish to thank my wife, Cheryl, for tolerating me when I tried out various pithy Yiddish expressions on her, and for her help in preparing it for publication and designing the cover. Thanks to Edit Kuper and Abe Fuchs for reviewing and correcting the Yiddish introduction. I also thank my two daughters, Sara and Rebecca, for testing some of these recipes, to make sure they really worked and were adaptable to modern ovens.

The Modern English-Yiddish Yiddish-English Dictionary, by Uriel Weinreich (YIVO Institute of Jewish Research) and *Yiddish, An Introduction to the Language, Literature & Culture*, by Sheva Zucker, *The Joys of Yiddish*, by Leo Rosten, and *Born to Kvetch*, by Michael Wex, were invaluable as references in preparing this book.

Prewar and some postwar photos have no attribution as I am unable to identify the photographer. The photo of our Saint John home was found in the New Brunswick official archives in Fredricton, and provided to me by Pat Craig. The photo of our first Passover seder in Saint John, New Brunswick and of the social gathering in Montreal were taken, I believe, by my cousin, Shimshe Perlmutter, (AKA Sam Perl), also an immigrant whose family arrived along with us soon after the war. He later became a well-known Montreal photographer (at Perl's Photo Studio on Victoria near Van Horne Avenue) during the second half of the 20th century. Except for the photo of Jerusalem *challahs* taken by Jake Levinson, most other photos and scans were taken by me or possibly my brother Percy.

Appendix

As a special bonus, I've included two glossaries, the first of food-related Yiddish words, and the second of Yiddish expressions, many filled with that special sarcasm that is expressed in Yiddish, for your education and entertainment. Both are transliterations of the Yiddish words, for ease of use and for my ease too. Many such glossaries are available on the web, but I have put these together as fully original material, although, how different can they be, really? Afer all, we're talking about the same language, aren't we? I've modified a few spellings for pronunciation and accuracy of meaning. Please use these lists responsibly, so as not to cause offense. Use while driving is perfectly acceptable, as long as you keep your eyes on the road, or if you are the driver's assistant in the back seat. Any mispronunciation is on your own head. Your mother or your bubby will let you know.

Yiddish Food Glossary

apricot	apricos
appetizer	forshpeiz
bagel	beigel
bake	baken
barley	gersht
beans	bubkes
beef	rinderent
beets	borik
berry	yagedeh
beverage	getrunk
blintz	blintz
blueberry	shvartze yagedeh
boil	oyfvelen
boil over	oyfloyfen
bottle	flaush
bread	broit

bread roll	zemel
broil	unterin fier
broth	yoich
buckwheat	kasheh
burn	bren
butter	pitter
cabbage	kroit
calf	kalb
cake	laikech
candy	tsukerul
carp	karp
carrot	meyer
carrot dish	tsimmes
celery	selerieh
cereal	kasheh
challah	challah
cheese	keyse
cherry	karsh
chicken	chun
chocolate	shokoladen
chop	kotlet
(to) chop	tsehaken
chopped meat	hak flaish
cinnamon	tzimering
cleaver	hakmesser
cook	oyskochen
cookbook	kochbuk
cookie	kichel
corn	pupshoy
cottage cheese	tzvorech
cream	shmeteneh
cup	kois
cut	einshniten
dairy	milckik
dish	shissel
drain	oisleidiken
duck	katchkeh
dumpling	kneidel
filled dough pockets	kreplech
egg	aye

egg white	viesel
egg yolk	gaylechel
eggplant	patlezhan
fat	shmaltz
fig	feig
fish	fish
flour	meyl
food	essen, shpeiz
fork	gupel
fruit	frucht
frying pan	skovrodeh
garlic	knobel
gizzard	pupik
glass	gluz
goose	ganden
grape	vientrob
grind	tsemulen
heart	hartz
hamantash	humentash
honey	honik
hungry	farhungert
intestine (stuffed)	kishke
jellied calves feet	petzeh
knife	messer
lamb	lemul
leavened bread	chometz
liqueur	lieker
liver	leyber
marrow	markh
matzah	matzeh
matzah ball	kneidel
meat	fleish(ik)
meringue	piano
milk	milkh
milk shake	mishmilkh
mince	tsehaken
mix	farmishen
nibble	nash
noodles	lokshen
nut	niss

nutmeg	mushkat
oil	boimel
onion	tzibel
orange	marantz
(bake) oven	bakryer, oyven
pan	pan
pancake	latke
paprika	paprikeh
parsley	petrishkeh
parsnips	pasternak
pastries	teiglech
peach	farshkeh
pear	baran
peas	arves
pepper	feffer
pie	peiy
plum	floim
pomegranate	milgrom
poppyseed	moun
pot	teppel
potato	kartofel
(mashed) potatoes	kartofel kasheh
pressure cooker	druktep
pretzel	veygeleh
prune	flom
pudding	kugel
raisin	rozhinkeh
raspberry	malehnes
rice	reiz
rye	koren
salt	zaltz
seasoning	viertzung
sieve	zippel
simmer	meliyen, unterziden
smell	reyach
smoke	royech
snack	iberbeisen
soak	veiken
soup	zup
sour pickle	zoyer oygerkeh

soy beans	soiyeh
spice	gevietz
spinach	spinat
spinach borsht	schav
stew (meat)	gedishechtz
stew (fruit, vegetable)	tzimmes
stir	dorchmishen
stove	oyven
strawberry	truskafkeh
stuffed cabbage	haloshkes
stuffed intestine	kishkeh
sturgeon	balik
sugar	tziker
sweet	zies
tablespoon	essleffel
taste	geshmak
tea	tay
teapot	chanik
teaspoon	leffeleh
tidbit	nasherei
toaster	tzuvroyner
tongue	tzung
trout	strongeh
turnip	brokveh
veal	kalb
vegetable soup	borscht
water	vasser
wheat	veitz
whiskey	bronfen
wine	vien
yeast	heiven

Glossary of Yiddish Words and Expressions

A

a bisel	a little
a biseleh	a very little
a broch!	a curse!!!
a broch tsu dir!	a curse on you!
a brocheh	a blessing
a deigeh hob ich	I don't care.
a farshlepteh krank	a chronic ailment
a feier zol im trefen	he should burn up!
a gezunt ahf dein kop	good health to you

(lit., good health on your head)

a glick ahf dir	good luck to you
a glick hot dir getrofen	lucky you
a nechtiker tug	forget it!
a shandeh un a charpeh	a shame
a shtik naches	a great joy
abi gezunt	may you be healthy
ahf tsores	in trouble
aidim	son-in-law
aleichem sholom	peace to you
alef-bais	alphabet
alevei!	it should happen to

me (to you)!

alter kucker	old man
an alter bakahnter	an old acquaintance
az och un vai!	too bad!

azoy	really?
azoy gait es!	so it goes!
azoy gich?	so soon?

B

bagruben	bury
baitsim	testicles
balbatish	respectable
balbusteh	housewife
bal toyreh	learned man, scholar
bareden yenem	to gossip
broygis	not on speaking terms
bashefen	a living
bashert	meant to be
behaimeh	animal(dull-witted person)
bentshen lecht	candle-lighting blessing
bes midrash	synagogue
billik	cheap, inexpensive
bist meshugeh?	are you crazy?
biteh	please
blondjen	be lost
bobkes	trifles
bohmer	bum
bris	circumcision
brucheh	blessing
bubby	grandmother

C

chaloshen	faint
chaloshes	faintness
chap arein	grab it and eat it! (while it's still there)
chap nisht!	don't grab
chas v'cholileh!	G-d forbid!
hazen	cantor
chazzer	pig (one who eats like a pig)
chazzerei	garbage
chai	life
cheiyeh	animal
chuchem	wise guy
chochmeh	wisdom
cholereh	curse, plague
chussen	bridegroom
chupeh	marriage canopy
chutzpeh	brazenness
chutzpedik	brazen

D

danken Got!	thank G-d!
daven	pray

deigeh nisht!	don't worry!
derech erets	the good path
dingen	bargain
dus gefelt mir	this pleases me
dus iz alts	that's all
drey mir nisht der kop!	don't mix me up
dreikop	scatterbrain
drek	feces
du fangst shoyn on?	you're starting up again?
dumkop	dunce
dybbuk	soul that invades a person, and must be exorcised.

E

efsher	maybe
einehoreh	the evil eye
ek velt	end of the world
emes	truth
er frest vi a ferd	he eats like a horse
er zitst oyfen shpilkes	he's restless (Lit., he sits on pins and needles)
er zol vaksen vi a tsibeleh, mit dem kop in drerd un die fiessen in himmel!	he should grow like an onion, with his head in the ground, and his feet in the air!

eretz yisroyel	Land of Israel
es brent mir ahfen hartz	I have a heartburn
es geyt nisht	it's not working
es gefelt mir	I like it
es iz a shandeh far di kinder!	it's a shame for the children!
es iz (tsi) shpeit	it is (too) late
es macht nisht oys	it doesn't matter
es past nisht	it is not seemly
es tut mir git	it does me good
es tut mir vey	it hurts me
es vert mir finster ofen oygen	I am fainting!
es vet gornisht helfen	nothing will help
es vet helfen vi a toiten bahnkes!	it won't help at all! (Lit., It will help like blood-cupping a dead person) (don't ask!)
ess gezunterhait	eat in good health
essen mitik	dine

F

fantazyor	fantasizer
farbissener	bitter person
farblondzhet	lost, bewildered
fardeyget	worried
fardinen	earn

fardrey zich dem kop!	drive yourself crazy!
fardroussen	sorrow
farfolen	lost
farfroyren	frozen
farkuckt	messed up (vulgar)
farmach dos moyl!	shut up!
farmatert	exhausted
farmisht	confused
farshtaist?	understand?
farshtoupt	stuffed
farshtunken	stinky
farshvitst	sweaty
ferd	horse
feigel (foigel)	bird
folg mich!	obey me!
fonfen	speak nasally
four gezunterhait!	travel in good health!
fortz	fart
frageh (froigeh)	question
freylech	joyous
freint	friend
fremder	stranger
fressen	eat ravenously
fresser	gourmand
froy	woman, wife
frimer/frumer mentsh	religious (person)

G

gey avek!	go away
gey feifen ahfen yam!	I have contempt for you (Lit. go whistle on the sea!)
gey gezunterheit!	go in good health
gey in drerd arein!	go to hell!
gey shoyn	come on, that can't be true!
galitsianer	native of Galicia
ganef	thief
gantseh megilleh	the whole deal
gantser mentsh	man of integrity
gatkes	long underwear
gebrochener	broken
gedainkst?	remember?
geferlech	terrible
geharget zolstu veren!	drop dead!
geliebteh	beloved
gelt	money
genaivisheh	underhanded
genug iz genug	enough is enough!
gesheft	business
geshmak	delicious
geshvollen	swollen

get	divorce
gezunt vi a ferd	strong as a horse
glezel tai	glass of tea
glick	luck
glitshik	slippery
gloib mir!	believe me!
gurnisht	nothing
Got in himmel!	G-d in heaven! (said
in despair)	
Got tsu danken	thank G-d
Gotteniu!	oh G-d! (anguished
cry)	
goy	non-Jew
goyeh	non-Jewish woman
greps	belch
grob	fat (overweight)
grober	coarse, crude
person	
groisser gornisht	good-for-nothing
g'vir	rich man

H

heymish punem	a friendly face
haken a tshanik	boring conversation
(lit., to bang on the tea-kettle)	

hak mir nisht in kop	stop talking my ear off (lit., stop banging my head)
handlen	do business
hartsveitik	heart ache
hert zich ein!	listen here!
hinten	behind
hiet zich!	look out!
hitsik	hothead
hob nisht kein deiges	don't worry

I

ich darf es ahf kapores	it's useless! (lit., I need it for a fowl sacrifice) (don't ask!!)
ich darf es vi a loch in kop!	I need it like a hole in the head!
ich veis	I know
ich veis nisht	I don't know
in a noveneh	for a change; once
in a blue moon	
in di alteh guteh tseiten!	in the good old days!
in miten drinen	in the middle of; suddenly

K

kaas	anger
kaftan	long coat
keyn eine horeh (keyne horah) - no evil eye!	
kalleh moid	girl of marriageable age
kapureh	atonement sacrifice, good for nothing
karger	meiser
kasheh	a tall tale
kashress	kosher condition
katzisher kop	forgetful (lit., cat brain)
(es) ken zein	maybe, could be
ketubbeh	marriage contract
kibbitz	offer unsolicited advice
kibbitzer	meddlesome spectator
kiddish	blessing over wine
kik im un!	look at him!
kim arein	come in
kinderlech	children
kleyner gornisht	a little nothing
klemt beim hartz	clutches at my heartstrings
klap mir nisht a tchanik	don't talk my ear off (lit. Don't bang a kettle)
klaperkeh	talkative woman
klop	punch or wallop
klotz (klutz)	klumsy person
kochedik	excitable

kop oif di pleytses! common sense! (lit., a
head on the shoulders!)

kopveytik	headache
koved	respect, honour
krank	sick
krankheit	illness
krechts	groan, moan
krechtser	complainer
kuntz	trick

kish mir in tuches! (vulgar) - kiss my ass!

k'velen	beam with delight or pride
k'vetsh	whine, complain

L

lang leben zolt ir!	live long! (and prosper)
lantsman	countryman
(a) leybediker	lively person

(a) leyben ahf dein kop!   praise (lit., long life
upon your head.)

leyben a chazerishen tog!   avaricious

le'chayim!   to life! (traditional Jewish
toast)

lemishkeh	milquetoast, bungler
leveiyeh	funeral
lig in drerd!	drop dead!
ligener	liar

litvak	Lithuanian
loch	hole
loz mich tzu rik!	leave me alone!
luftmentsh	impractical person
loch in kop	a hole in the head
(e.g. "I need this like a loch in kop")	

M

machen a leyben	make a living
(groiser) macher	big shot, dealmaker
mameniu	my little girl (term of endearment)
megilleh	long story
meydel	unmarried young woman
meydeleh	little girl
meyven	expert, connoisseur
makeh	plague, curse
mamzer	bastard, disliked person
mashgiach	supervisor of kashruth
mazel tov	good luck
me ken lecken di finger!	it's delicious!
me lost nisht leyben!	they bother you!
me redt zich oys dos hartz!	talk your

heart out! (spill your guts!)

mechayeh	pleasure
mein bobbeh's ta'am	old fashioned taste!
mentsh	a person worthy of respect
meshpucheh	extended family
meshugass	madness
meshugeh	crazy
meshugeh ahf toit!	really crazy!
meshugeneh	crazy woman
meshugener	crazy man
mir zogt	it is said
metziah	a bargain, gift
mies	ugly
mieskeit	ugly thing or person.
miet	tired
mikveh	ritual bath
minyen	quorum of ten necessary for joint prayer
mertsishem	G-d willing
mitzveh	good deed
mogen Duvid	Star of David
moisheh kapoyer	A person who does everything backwards

moyel	man who performs circumcisions
mutek	brave

N

na!	here! take it
naches	joy, especially because of children's accomplishments
nacht	night
nar	fool
narener!	you fool!
narish	foolish
narishkeit	foolishness
nebech	pity, unlucky person
nebbish	a nobody, simpleton
(a) nechtiker tog! (lit., a yesterday's day)	forget it! nonsense!
neshoumeh	soul, spirit
neshomeleh	sweetheart
niskusheh	satisfactory
nisht do gedacht!	it shouldn't happen!
nisht gedeiget	don't worry
nisht getrofen!	wrong, not found
nisht gut	not good, lousy
nisht naitik	not necessary
nishtgutnick	no-good person

nishtikeit!	a nobody!
nit ahin, nit aher	neither here nor there
nishtu gedacht!	G-d forbid!
nit gedacht gevorn	it shouldn't come to pass
nit keyn farshloffener	a lively person
nit kosher	impure food
nit heint, nit morgen!	not today, not tomorrow!
nit farvous!	for what?, you're welcome!
noch nisht	not yet
nor Got veist	only G-d knows
nu?	so? well?
nu, shoyn!	come on! Let's get going! Aren't you finished?
nudnik	nuisance, obnoxious person
nudje	annoying person
nudjen	annoy
nuchshlepper	hanger-on, unwanted follower

O

och un vai!	it's terrible
ohmeyn	amen
oyfen shpilkes	restless, nervous
ois-shteler	show-off
oungebloizen	conceited peevish
oungebloizener	stuffed shirt
oungematert	tired out
oungepatshket	cluttered, disordered, messy, kitschy
oungeshtupt	rich
oungevarfen	cluttered
ounzaltsen	bribe (lit., to salt)
oupgekrochen	shoddy
oupgeloizener	careless dresser
oupgenart	cheated
oupnarer	cheat
oupnarerei	deception
ouber yetzt?	so what's next?
ourem-man	poor man
ouremkeit	poverty
oy!	oh! (with a touch of self-pity added)
oy vey!, oy veis mir!	oh my, woe is me
oyfen himmel a yarid!	much ado about nothing!
oyfgekumener	upstart
oy, gevalt!	cry of anguish

oys shiddech	cancelled betroval
oysgedart	skinny
oysgehorevet	exhausted
oysgematert	tired out, worn out
oysgepatcht	overdressed
oysgeshpreit	spread out
oysvarf	outcast, bad person

P

peygeren zol er!	he should drop dead!
parmeylech!	slowly
parnosseh	livelihood, business
parveh	neutral food,
neither milchidik (dairy) nor flaishidik (meat)	
paskudnik, paskudnyak	disgusting fellow
patsh	smack
patshkes arim	wastes time
pipek (pupik)	belly button
pishachtz	urine
pisher	male infant, pee-er
pisk	loudmouth
pitsel	tiny
pluggen	work hard
plats	explode, fall apart
prost	coarse, common

proster mentsh	common man
ptsha	cows feet in jelly (supposedly a delicacy) (don't ask!)
punim	face
pushkeh	charity box

S

seychel	common sense
se brent nisht!	don't get excited! (lit., it's not on fire!)
shabbes goy	gentile who does duties forbidden for a Jew on the Sabbath (don't ask!)
shadchen	matchmaker
sheygitz	non-Jewish boy
sheyn vi di levuneh	pretty as the moon
sheyn vi di zibbent himmel (velten)	beautiful as heaven
sheyneh meydel	pretty girl
sheinkeit	beauty
sheytel	wig
shalach muhnes	sweets sent for Purim
sholom	peace
shammes	sexton; candle used to light other candles on a menorah
sheymevdik	bashful, shy

shep naches	derive sublime pleasure and pride, especially from children or grandchildren (need you ask?)
shidech	marriage match (arranged) (don't ask!)
shikker	drunkard
shikseh	non-Jewish girl
shiva	traditional seven day mourning period
shlang	snake; penis (vulgar)
shlecht	bad
shlemiel	clumsy person
shlep	drag, pull
shlepper	free-loader, leach
shlimazel	unlucky person; one with perpetual bad luck (it is said that the shlemiel spills the soup on the shlimazel!)
shlug dein kop in vant	bang your head on the wall
shluggen mit Got	fight City Hall! (lit., go fight with God.)
shlugen	to fight, to beat up
shloss	lock
shlosser	mechanic
shlub	slob
shlump	unkempt person
shmaltzy	corny

shmatteh	rag
shmatteh trade	clothing industry
shmeer	smear, coat
shmegegge	oaf
shmekel	boor, idiot, penis- (vulgar)
shmendrik	similar to shmoe and shlemiel, penis (vulgar)
shmo(e)	see shlemiel or shmendrick
shmuck	boor, penis (vulgar)
shmontses	baubles
shmouz	discuss
shmuts	dirt
shmutzik	dirty, soiled
shnapps	whiskey, same as bronfen
shneider	tailor
shnell	quick, quickly
shnuk	a patsy, a sucker, a sap, easy-going, person easy to impose upon, gullible
shnorrer	a beggar who makes pretensions to respectability; sponger, a parasite
shnur	daughter-in-law
shoymer	watchman, guard
shoyn fargessen?	already forgotten?
shoyn genug!	that's enough!

shpigel nei (lit. mirror-new)	brand-new (lit. mirror-new)
shpilkes	pins and needles
shpitsfinger	toes
shreklecheh zach (frightening)	a terrible thing
shtark, shtarker	strong, a powerhouse
shtark vi a ferd	stong as a horse
schav (borsht)	cold spinach or sorrel soup
shtik	piece; a special ability or characteristic
shtik drek	shit-head (lit. piece of shit)
shtik naches	a great joy
shtikel	small piece
shtiklech	tricks; small pieces
shtrudel	strudel
shtunk	a stink
shtup	push; have sex (vulgar)
shul	synagogue
shuleh	school
shvachkeit	weakness
shvegerin	sister-in-law
shvungerin	pregnant
shver	father-in-law; difficult, heavy
shviger	mother-in-law

shvindel	dizzy
shvitz	sweat, steam bath
shvuger	brother-in-law
sidder	Jewish prayer book
simcheh	joyous occasion
sitzfleish	patience
smudgeh	a stain

T

ta'am	flavor, good taste
tahkeh	really, truly
tahkeh a metsieh	really a bargain! (sarcasm)
tallis	fringed prayer-shawl
Talmud	set of books interpreting

Jewish law, written by a group of rabbis after
the exile of the Jews from Israel in the time of
the Romans

Talmud Torah	Jewish school for children
Tashlich	Act of the casting away

sins during the Jewish New Year (usually bread
thrown into running water) (again, don't ask)

tateh	father
tateh-mameh	parents
tateleh	dear little boy (term of

endearment)

tatenui	father dear

teier	dear, expensive
teiyerinkeh!	dearest
temp	stupid
temper kop	stupid person
tit mir nisht kein toives	don't do me any favours
tuches	buttocks, ass
tuches-lecker	brown-noser, sycophant
toig ahf kapures!	good for nothing! worthless
traif	forbidden food, non-kosher
toiveh	favour
trenen	to tear
trug gezunterhait!	wear it in good health!
trombenik	a bum
tsim gezint!	to your health! (said after a sneeze)
tzaddik	righteous person
tzeblondget	lost, mixed up
tzedukeh	charity
tzedrait	crazy, screwy, mixed up
tzedraiter kop	crazy person
tzegait zich	melts
tzemisht	confused
tzhatchkeh	toy, doodad

tzhepen	to annoy,pinch, poke, or to jab
tsim gezunterheit	to your good health
tsitskeh	breast or nipple
tsures	troubles
tsum glik, tsum shlimazel	for better, for worse
tumel	confusion or noise
tumler	agitator, troublemaker
tut vai dos harts	heartbroken
tzitzis	fringes attached to the four corners of the tallis
tzufil	too much!

V

vey is mir! - woe is me!

Y

yachneh	gossipy woman
yarmelkeh	traditional Jewish head covering, also called a kippah, worn by men
yashir koyech	may your strength continue (said to honour someone)
yenems	someone else's

yener velt	the world to come, the world after death
yenteh	woman who puts her nose into other people's business; female blabbermouth
yeshiveh	talmudic academy
yeshiveh bocher	student of talmudic academy
yeshuvnik	farmer, man of the countryside
yichus	family background
yiddisher kop	smart person
yiskor	prayer for the dead
Yom Kippur	Day of Atonement
yontefdik	festive, in the holiday spirit
yuhrtseit	anniversary of death
Yukel	buffoon
Yung mit bainer!	young and strong
yung	young

Z

zaftig or zaftik	juicy, a plump or fulsome (woman), (Lit. squeezable)
zei shtil	be quiet
zelbeh	same

zolt helfen az a toiten bankes   it's useless
(Lit.: it will help like bloodblistering for a dead
man) (again, don't ask)
zug mir nisht kein kashes   don't tell me
any tall tales

You will find a much more comprehensive (and fun) lexicon of
Yiddish words, terms, and expressions, with plenty of explanations
and examples of usage, in Leo Rosten's *The Joys of Yiddish*.

א אָ אַ ב בּ בֿ ג ד ה ו וו וי ז ח ט י יי ײַ כּ כ ך ל מ ם נ ן ס ע פּ פֿ פ ף צ ץ ק ר ש שׂ ת תּ

www.ingramcontent.com/pod-product-compliance
Lightning Source LLC
LaVergne TN
LVHW091308080426
835510LV00007B/421